MR HARRINGTON

GN00789597

ASTRONAUT
SUNITA WILLIAMS

ASTRONAUT SUNITA WILLIAMS

ACHIEVER EXTRAORDINAIRE

Capt. S. Seshadri
Aradhika Sharma

Foreword by
Wg Cdr (Retd) Rakesh Sharma
The First Indian Astronaut

Preface by
Bonnie Pandya
Sunita Williams' Mother

Rupa & Co

Typeset in 12 pt. Calisto
Mindways Design
1410 Chiranjiv Tower,
43 Nehru Place
New Delhi 110 019

Printed in India by
Rekha Printers Pvt. Ltd.
A-102/1 Okhla Industrial Area, Phase-II
New Delhi-110 020

Contents

Acknowledgement

The authors would like to acknowledge **Roopinder Singh** without whose guidance and unstinting support this work would not have been possible and **The Pandya Family** who patiently answered all our queries and enriched this book, factually and visually.

Foreword

I am privileged to introduce this book as it records the remarkable life and times of Sunita Williams. This is the true life story of a woman of many parts: Naval Aviator and Helicopter Pilot, later Test Pilot; Professional Naval Diver; Swimmer; Charity Fund raiser; Animal lover; Marathon runner and now, Astronaut and world record holder!

Sunita comes across as an ordinary person who realised her extraordinary potential by sheer dint of hard work and a 'can-do' attitude. She tasted success by steeling herself to go that extra mile, explore her personal limits and become an inspiring example to those who aspire to follow her footsteps. She achieved this with the support of her close-knit family and friends.

The book provides readers with a snapshot of Sunita's achievements; her incredible journey from childhood, right through her professional career and ends with her noteworthy contribution towards the American Space Programme as a crew member of STS 116, aboard the Space Shuttle 'Atlantis'.

A truly inspiring story.

Wg Cdr (Retd) Rakesh Sharma
Research Cosmonaut, India
Soyuz T-10/Salyut-7
20 June 2007

Preface

Cmdr. Sunita Lyn Pandya Williams USN was born in Cleveland, Ohio, USA, on 19 September 1965. Her father and my husband is Deepak N. Pandya, M.D., from Mongrol, India. My name is Bonnie Zalokar Pandya and I am Suni's mother. She has an older brother, Jay Thomas Pandya and an older sister, Dina Ann Pandya. We all moved to the area around Boston by Suni's first birthday. Although the family was not overjoyed at the news of moving away from their grandparents, various aunts, uncles and cousins, they supported Deepak's professional endeavours and relocated.

While Deepak's medical career was blossoming, so were the children. I engaged all three in various musical and athletic activities. I loved to bake while the children attended school and they would come home to find freshly baked cookies and cakes. The children would do their homework and then they would all pile in the car for the drive to swimming practice. During this two-hour wait, I would usually keep myself busy watching them swim and doing needlework. Since Deepak was, and is, a strict vegetarian, I would cook two meals—one Indian and one Slovenian. The children were encouraged to try both.

As time went by, I started teaching needlework at night school. As the children grew older, I started working full time while still taking the children to morning swimming practice at 5.30 a.m. By this time, Jay got his driver's license and was able to drive everyone to the afternoon practice. And so life in the Pandya household continued on this rigorous schedule. All the neighbours were amazed at the comings and goings of the Pandya family—we were always on the move.

After Jay went off to college at the United States Naval Academy and Dina went off to school at Smith College, things still didn't settle down. There were always medical colleagues visiting from Europe and the United States who stayed at our house while working with Deepak. I went to night school to get my degree in Business and Sunita kept swimming and studying. During one summer, she worked as a swimming instructor.

New England became our home and the whole family loved living in the Boston area. There were great musical plays to attend, exciting Patriots and Red Sox games to watch, and rivers, lakes and an ocean to swim in.

In the Fall, everyone loved camping in New Hampshire and Maine and to see the magical leaves turn from green to various hues of red, yellow, and orange. The children loved the corn stalks, the pumpkins and the Halloween costumes I made for them. They loved Thanksgiving and Christmas Holidays as well as Diwali and the various Indian holidays when I made *gugrah, halwa, jalebi* and *gulab jamun*. The family enjoyed waking up to a fresh carpet of snow in the cold winter mornings. Sometimes Dina and Jay looked out the window and thought: "Oh! No swimming today", but there was Suni, getting on her swimming suit and waiting for everyone to get going.

The summers were especially fun since we were able to go camping more frequently. Jay and I would connect the camper to the car. Suni and Dina would pack up the food and clothing, we would take our dog and drive over to the hospital and pick Deepak up from work and continue on our trip. The children's cousins would come for a couple of weeks and all would go sailing and swimming in the ocean.

Everyone looked forward to spending time at our house. We would have a 4th of July party when I would cook and bake and the children would play volleyball and croquet and have a wonderful time with family and friends. The children especially loved packing a picnic lunch and going on the train to Boston to see the Independence Day Celebration and especially the fireworks. Usually, they would climb up a tree by the Charles River to get a better view of the fireworks and musicians playing patriotic songs.

Yes, indeed, Boston was a wonderful place for the children to grow up in. Ours is a lovely family and we have many great friends. The children had wonderful teachers who made learning a fun and positive experience for them. Through Deepak's friends, relatives and colleagues, the children were able to experience many different cultures. If I may add, the children are fortunate to have parents from two different backgrounds, who came together and stayed together to enhance their lives with their hard work and experiences. Jay, Dina and Suni are unique in this respect.

Deepak soon rose to become Professor of Anatomy and Neurobiology at the Boston University School of Medicine. His investigations into the anatomy of the cerebral cortex at the Harvard Neurological Unit at the Boston City Hospital, the Aphasia Research Center of the Boston Veterans Administration Hospital, and the Bedford Veterans Administration Hospital span four decades and an international field of collaborators. For this work he has received the Cajal Club Discoverer and Explorer Awards and the Signoret Award. Throughout this time he has actively practiced clinical medicine and taught generations of students.

Cmdr. Sunita Lyn Pandya Williams, USN is a remarkable woman. We have gladly shared her life's story with the authors, Aradhika Sharma and Capt. S. Seshadri, who have put it together for you to read.

Bonnie Pandya
20 June 2007
Cape Cod, MA, USA

Conquering the Elements

Sunita Lyn Williams is now back from her six month billet at the International Space Station, where she served as a flight engineer. As a member of NASA's Expedition-14 crew, Sunita Williams established a world record for women, through four spacewalks totalling 29 hours and 17 minutes of 'Extravehicular Activity', as spacewalk is unromantically termed by NASA.

Sunita is an icon and looking back at her life, to date, there are many experiences and influences that have contributed to the idol she has become—which have made her an ideal candidate for the career in which she is excelling.

- From her father she learned the values of simple living and spiritual happiness, of family bonding and the awesome beauty of Nature.

- From her mother she derived her strength and her great beauty, learned to be organised, and understood the ever-fresh feeling of fun, friends and creativity.
- From her brother she understood the need to work hard, to succeed in studies and in sports.
- From her sister she got a friend for life, realised compassion in people and learned many other wonderful things by emulating her.
- From her competitors in swimming she imbibed the thrill of pitting her physical energies against peers and the importance of dedication, commitment, lifelong fitness and health.
- From the Naval Academy she developed leadership and survival skills, learned to be a team player and to work without fear or favour in a male dominated environment.
- From Navy Diving she learnt many practical skills (working and living underwater—which is very much like living and working in space) that would prepare her for her career as an astronaut.
- From being a Test Pilot she worked towards taking on challenges, honing problem-solving skills, dexterity, the spirit of camaraderie and courage.
- From her husband she learned the value of friendship, love, respect and security.
- From Gorby, her beloved Jack Russell terrier, she learned the value of humour, companionship, peace and joy.

This is how Sunita (Pandya) Williams' parents sum up her journey in life.

This is the story of an 'ordinary woman' who has reached the pinnacle of achievement, supported by an extraordinary family.

It was in April 2007 that Kapish Mehra, Publisher, Rupa and Co., asked Captain Seshadri (Sesh) and me to do a book on Sunita Williams. Blithely, we agreed, though I did voice the doubt: 'Where are we going to get the material from? She isn't anywhere close by and neither is her family. I mean, her folks are halfway round the globe, in America and she . . . well, she is halfway up to the skies!'

'No problem, don't worry, we'll do it,' was Sesh's characteristic response. And I was happy to believe him.

Thus began our research on Sunita. We visited long forgotten bookstores in our respective cities (Sesh lives in Chennai, and I in Chandigarh), browsed through all the publications where we were likely to find information on her and Googled every site that even mentioned 'Sunita Williams'. In the meantime, I called every friend and acquaintance I had in order to ask if anyone could get us the contact details either of the Pandya family or of Michael Williams, Sunita's husband. Sesh did the same, though with much more dignity, I suspect.

Finally, I got a call from our friend Roopinder Singh (whose assistance and contribution to this book has been invaluable), jubilantly yelling: 'I got it! I got it!'

'What have you got now?' was my grumpy response, reminded of Archimedes' 'Eureka'!

'Dr Deepak Pandya's official phone number and mail ID,' he said.

After the two of us had jubilated enough and congratulated ourselves on our brilliance and enterprise, I called Sesh, who was promptly designated to carry out the correspondence. After days of anticipated reply from Dr Pandya and not receiving it, we learnt to our disappointment that he was not in Boston where he has established himself as a neuroanatomist of repute.

Now we were dependent only on the World Wide Web, which seemed to grow narrower by the minute. We had already chalked out the master plan for the book and started working on it. We even completed our manuscript and sent it to the publisher for approval. And *then* came a call from Sesh, which started with his reading out 'Dear Capt. Seshadri. Apologies for the delay in replying to your mail. I have been away for the past seven months.' It was a mail from Dr Pandya. My squeals of excitement had my office colleagues gathering around me to enquire the cause of my joyousness.

Quickly, we put together a questionnaire and mailed it to Dr Pandya. A few days later, Sesh called again. 'We've got the response,' he said, while still in the process of reading the mail. 'Good Lord! (this was not the term he actually used) There's pages and pages and PAGES of it *and* they are sending us pictures too!'

The Pandya family, Deepak, Ursaline (Sunita's mother) and Dina (her sister) had got together and sent us such exhaustive material, so many personal details about Sunita and the family; we were left with no choice but to re-write the whole book. The icing on the cake was when we got a message from Sunita herself from SPACE, through her sister Dina about a few things that she wanted included in the book.

Perusing the material that the family had sent, we were totally awed by the immense and loving support that Bonnie (Ursaline) and Deepak gave their children. Sunita is exploring space today but the roots had been planted deep by her parents and siblings, who also gave her the wings to fly.

Writing this book has been an exciting venture for Sesh and me. The best part has been in exploring a life so rich, so full, so committed, so focussed and so disciplined as to be exemplary. We started out with looking for an icon, but as we researched, we came across a person who was clear-headed, hard working, goal oriented and loving. And a family that is responsible for nurturing this person who is now an icon!

Aradhika Sharma

Earth

On 10 December 2006, at 7.17 a.m. Indian Standard Time, the space shuttle Discovery lifted off from Kennedy Space Centre, Houston, Texas, USA. Aboard it, along with the other flight crew, was Sunita Williams. Two days later, 354 kilometres in the space above Bangladesh, she entered the International Space Station (ISS), the abode where she would live for the next six months. 'Tally ho! on the new home,' was her first message to earth.

The ISS is a research facility currently being assembled in outer space. It is conceived as an effort to provide insights into outer space and also act as a launch pad for future lunar and Mars missions.

The ISS has been continuously inhabited since 2 November 2000 and is serviced by the Russian Soyuz and Progress and by the American space shuttle orbiters.

It has also been the destination of the first five space-tourists. The project was announced in 1993, after the end of the Cold War and the space wars standoff, and is to be completed by 2010 at an estimated total cost of US$ 130 billion (approximately Rs 530,000 crore).

For Sunita, the sudden change from earth to space was tremendous. As the astronauts floated around weightless, she had to be pulled down and held firmly for a group photograph. One of the first things she did was to have fellow astronaut, Joan Higginbotham, cut her ponytail. The shorn hair was donated to Locks of Love, a US based charitable organisation that provides hair prosthesis to disadvantaged children suffering from permanent hair loss caused by cancer, radiation treatment or burns.

What made her decide to donate her hair? 'I was inspired by a friend who did the same thing, and I thought, wow, that is a good idea. I am just happy that I am healthy and had long hair and could give it to someone else. I always knew that it would be a bad idea to have long hair up here getting caught in the fans and getting in each other's way. So the idea to cut my hair came as soon as I was assigned to this flight. I sort of wanted a picture of what it looked like when I had really long hair in space and so I did get that picture taken and I knew I was going to cut it off in the shuttle before I came here, so that I didn't get the station all full of hair.'

Her long black locks, now shorn, indicate her Indian origin—her father, Dr Deepak Pandya is a Gujarati.

Gujarati Father, Slovenian Mother

'I was born in Mangrol, a little town on the west coast of Saurashtra in India, on 6 December 1932. My father was a businessman in Bombay. My parents were highly spiritual people.' Unfortunately, his father died when Deepak was just two years old and his mother passed away by the time he was thirteen. Deepak went to school in Julhason village in north Gujarat, and later in Ahmedabad. He completed his professional studies from Surat, where he received his medical degree in 1957. He then worked as an intern at the V.S. Hospital, Junagadh, for a year.

Deepak sailed to England and then to the USA in 1958 for further studies. Incidentally, Deepak is closely related to the late Haren Pandya, Gujarat's former Home Minister, who was killed in 2004. The Pandya family proudly recalls that Sunita's first visit to Gujarat was for the sacred thread ceremony of Haren Pandya. This ceremony, *upanayana*, traditionally took place when a boy left home to live with his guru; however, today it is conducted when a boy reaches puberty.

In the US, Deepak did his internship and residency training in medicine at the Euclid General Hospital, Ohio. It was here that he met Bonnie Ursaline Zalokar, who is

3

of Slovenian origin—her grandparents are from there, although her parents were born in Cleveland, Ohio. Bonnie's grandfather and father owned a delicatessen, a shop selling ready-to-eat food products. The family was highly regarded among the Slovenian community. In her father's family were three girls and four boys. Her mother's family comprised six sisters. 'We were a very happy family and got together every weekend to play music, play games and eat delicious Slovenian food made by the women of the families.'

Bonnie had two brothers and a sister. 'My sister is a teacher and has three daughters. They all live in Colorado. My brother Tony was a Marine and served in Vietnam. He died in a motorcycle accident when he was thirty-three. My brother Hank retired from General Motors, a major American corporation.' Both brothers played football and basketball and had scholarships to college. The entire family was musically inclined and played musical instruments. Her sister played the piano, she the accordion, Hank the saxophone and clarinet, and Tony the guitar. Her father played the banjo and her mother the piano. Together, they made up a band and jammed as a family band!

Bonnie recalls: 'I had a scholarship to college on my music but decided instead to go to X-Ray Technician School at Euclid General Hospital. I met Deepak there. He was a resident physician in the same hospital. We got married and gave birth to Jay, Dina and then Suni (short for Sunita).

'We decided to move to Boston, MA after Suni was one year old, to continue with the research work which my husband had started at the Case-Western Reserve Institute in Cleveland, Ohio. At first, we were not too happy and thought we would move back to Ohio after a year. As time went by, however, the kids got involved in different activities and we grew to love Massachusetts.'

Deepak had become a naturalised American citizen just a year before Sunita was born. He taught at Harvard Medical School and Boston University Medical School and worked at several hospitals in the Boston area. The famous hub of education and medicine on the east coast of America was to be the family's home for the next several years.

Sunita has happy memories and impressions of the town she grew up in. 'It's a great little town. There were about five hundred kids in my high school graduating class, but it seems like you know everybody in a town that size. And it is a great sports town to grow up in.'

Growing up in Needham

Sunita went to school at the Hillside Elementary School from kindergarten to the sixth grade; from where she shifted to Newman Junior High School to study from the seventh to the ninth grade; after which she went to Needham High School from the tenth to the twelfth grade. Her favourite teacher was Mrs Angela DiNapoli, who taught her in the fifth grade.

Years later, when Sunita went to NASA for an interview, she decided to take a jog around the grounds after the interview. As she was jogging, a car pulled up and one of the interviewers jumped out. 'There is someone here that wants to talk to you,' she said. Lo and behold! It was Mrs DiNapoli. She had been down at NASA getting information for a class that she was teaching about space at Needham! Sunita couldn't believe her eyes. Since then, they have been communicating regularly with one another.

Suni has returned to her school several times to talk to students about space. Nearly seventy students from Mrs DiNapoli's class recently interacted with Sunita via Polycom, a videoconferencing device at Babson College, MA. They saw their favourite astronaut on the ISS. NASA had set up the videoconference and it was supposed to be for a fifteen-minute visit, but Sunita stayed on for close to forty-five minutes.

She also gave the students a tour of the space station, which is about the size of an airliner. She wowed the kids by doing flips and letting Gatorade drink float out of a straw and form a red, sugary bubble. Then she slurped it up midair! The children were simply fascinated. Among them was eleven year-old Rebecca Phillips who feels a special connection with Sunita. Rebecca swims competitively, as Sunita did as a child, and their fathers are both doctors.

Sunita loved sports, especially swimming. 'I spent a lot of time before school and after school, swimming. I would contribute whatever discipline and direction I had to competitive swimming. It takes up a lot of your time and then you're trying to fit it in, doing your homework and having a social life as you're growing up.'

As a child, Sunita would come home from school, have a snack and do her homework. She would continue with her homework while her parents drove her to swimming practice, which was about forty-five minutes from their home. After practice, she would come home and get back to her books.

Bonnie recollects: 'When we drove to swimming practice she always quizzed me on the artists (whose songs were being broadcast on the radio). Who is singing? What's the name of this song? I remember that she liked Bruce Springsteen, James Taylor, Steely Dan, Todd Rungren, Dan Fogelberg, Queen, Elton John, Chicago, America, Supertramp, Fleetwood Mac, Peter Gabriel, Bruce Hornsby and the Range, Steve Winwood, U2, Aerosmith and Robert Palmer.'

Swimming, Seriously

One summer Sunita was doing a job as a lifeguard at Wellesley College, one of the most famous Ivy League institutions for women in the US. It was a backbreaking routine. After returning from her morning swimming practice, she would get on her bike and ride to Wellesley College, about thirty minutes from their house. She would ride home for lunch, get back to her lifeguard duties and finally ride back home again.

Deepak would take her back in the evening for swimming practice. After practice, she would again go to Wellesley College and help with the special-needs kids who were attending camp there!

Sunita was very serious about her swimming. 'Usually, at the end of August, the kids got two weeks off from swimming before they went back to school during fall. We made it a point to take them camping as much as we could. One of the camping trips was in New Hampshire where we loved to go and climb the White Mountains and swim in the Swift River and go under the waterfalls. One time, we were enjoying our trip when it started pouring. We couldn't close up the camper to return home and there was a swim meet the next day. Suni insisted that we leave everything there and drive the two hundred miles back to the swim meet. So we left everything there and drove home so she could attend the swim meet. The following day my son and I went up again to New Hampshire to pack up the camper and bring it home,' recollects Deepak.

Her best friends were swimmers who came from all over New England to swim with her at the Harvard

University pool in Cambridge, MA. They were like family since they saw each other twice everyday.

Sunita still keeps contact with many of them. She lost track of some of her close friends as a result of her military commitment and travels but since her recent accomplishments and news about her work in the space programme, some of her old friends have contacted her parents for her address or email.

Sunita was very excited to hear from them and knows that they were asking about her. She is looking forward to seeing them on her return to earth. She always had lots of great friends and has always understood the value of friendship. In general, people love to be around her because she is positive and happy and likes to have fun, says her proud mother.

One of Sunita's best school friends is Pam Chen, a veterinarian, who she still sees and corresponds with. Another good friend is Charlie Lownes who lives in Ohio. Both attended her launch in December 2006 to the ISS. 'It was very special to Suni that they were there and to them for being there to see their close friend do such a remarkable thing. Some of the parents of the swimmers have contacted me since they found out Suni is an astronaut. They all said they knew Suni would go far. She was always pushing herself to the limit. She could have gone to Columbia University or Yale and when she chose the US Naval Academy they weren't surprised by her decision to once again push herself to becoming one of the only hundred women in her class of one thousand, with only about half of them graduating,' says her father.

Sukhadi and *Pakora* on Weekends

Bonnie tells us of the favourite family pastimes: 'We liked to play bridge. Since Suni was the youngest she was not interested in playing. However, when we needed a dummy, she always volunteered. It was the same with tennis. I loved playing tennis but Suni was not interested. However, she would come and get the ball for us if we hit it out of the court.

'Whenever we had a free day, we would pack up the camper and go camping someplace. Suni and Dina would love to bake cookies with me. We had several litters of puppies and we always played with them and took them for walks. Deepak would take the kids to MIT to spiritual meetings. He would take them to his research lab at the City Hospital in Boston and talked to them about his research.

'Deepak liked to make *sukhadi* and *pakora* on weekends and we all pitched in cutting up brown sugar for the *sukhadi* and vegetables for the *pakora*. We listened to Indian music and ate our snacks. The kids also like to sit on the floor Indian style and eat Indian food with their hands—something American kids don't often do.

Sunita, at age one.

Sunita and Dina wearing ballet recital costumes.

Sunita after she wrote the word 'Ram' in Hindi in the sand.

Sunita at about age seven.

The girls bake a
gingerbread house for
the holidays.

Sunita at a swimming meet
representing Bernal's Gators
(12th grade).

Sunita receiving her
High School Diploma
in 1983.

Sunita with fellow
plebes at the United
States Naval Academy
(USNA) Annapolis,
Maryland, USA.

Sunita with classmates
at USNA.

With two of her bridesmaids, Debbie and Vicki, from USNA ready to attend a formal event.

Climbing the Herndon Monument at the end of Plebe Summer (1983).

Sunita and Dina at USNA after Plebe Summer in 1983.

Cycling to win a triathalon.

A swimming portrait,
Captain of USNA women's swimming
team during her senior year.

Running cross-country at USNA.

USNA cross-country team.

Sunita as a helicopter pilot.

The two sisters at a wedding in India.

Elephant ride during the family's trip to India in 1998.

At the Taj Mahal,
Dr. Deepak Pandya, Sunita, Dina and Denish Raval.

Getting her 'Wings'. Sunita's husband-to-be, Michael Williams, is on the left.

Receiving the Navy Diver insignia.

In parachute jumping gear.

A friend pins on her 'Airborne Wings'.

Preparing for a dive at special ops diver training in Panama City, Florida.

Group photo of jump school class at Ft. Benning, Georgia.

Sunita, flanked by sister Dina and brother Jay, at her wedding.

With her father.

Proud parents, Bonnie and Deepak.

Sunita and Michael's
wedding in Woods Hole,
MA, in 1989.

Sunita and husband Michael.

Bonnie, Coal, Gorby
and Sunita.

Trekking together:
Sunita and Dina.

Celebrating
Sunita's 40th
birthday in
September 2005.

FORTY ISN'T OLD
IF YOUR A TREE

Sunita sharing her experiences with school students...

... and joining them for a group photograph.

A formal portrait of United States Naval Academy's 3rd Company.

Proudly wearing the American flag. A family portrait to mark 40 years of Deepak and Bonnie's marriage. From left: Sunita, Mike, Jay, Deepak, Bonnie, Anna (Jay's wife), Coal and Dina in Cape Cod, MA.

'We took them to St. Joseph's Church where they all received their first communion and confirmation and went to mass every Sunday as a family. Dad would bring the *Bhagvad Gita* and would read while the rest of us attended the church ceremony.

'We also loved sailing. We would go to Boston where they gave sailing lessons on the Charles River. We all learned how to sail there. We also had a sunfish, canoe and a windsurfer. We all sailed in the nearby Lake Waban in Wellesley.'

Fun Family

Many incidents together create a collage of experiences the family had together, and here is how Deepak, Bonnie and Dina recount them.

'Once we went to a theme park in New Hampshire, called Storyland. When we got there the park was closed and the kids had wanted to see it very badly. We let them climb over the fence to get a look. They got scared and ran back and climbed over the fence but left Suni sitting on top of the fence crying. We had to rescue her. She was five at the time.

'Some other places we camped at included Yellowstone National Park, Cheyenne, Wyoming, and the Badlands of South Dakota, Price Edward Island, Canada; New York City, Washington DC, Florida and Disney World and various other places on Cape Cod and New England. These trips were some of the fondest childhood memories for Suni and all of us. All of the kids talk about these trips today and continue to camp with their own friends and family. Recently, Suni and Dina hiked and camped the last hundred miles on the Appalachian Trail in Maine. It was challenging but they both encouraged and supported each other and did the entire hike in nine days.

'Once when I was working, my husband took Suni and four of her girl friends camping on Cape Cod. He called me to complain about them. They were all bringing sand into the camper and he had to continuously sweep the floor. Then Suni made pancakes for them for breakfast. She had long hair and as she was bending to turn the pancakes her hair caught on fire. No wonder, Deepak declared that he was not going camping with the girls again!

✧

'Another incident was when we camped in Maine. We brought along my sister's two girls and another cousin. All in all we had six kids with us. It was hot and they all wanted to swim across to an island. First my son Jay jumped in and swam, followed by Dina, Suni, the rest of the girls and finally I swam across to make sure they were all okay. However, we gave my husband all our clothes and shoes and left him on the other side. We then hiked all around in our bare feet and bathing suits. He finally met up with us after an hour carrying all our clothes and shoes. They always remember how much fun we had although the water temperature was ice cold (about fifty-five degrees) when we did our swim.

✧

'When we heard about the Boston Harbor Marathon Swim from the Boston Light to the aquarium, about fifteen miles, Suni was determined to do it along with her brother Jay. The day before, we went to Boston harbour to check out the course and take a boat ride through the course. The water was loaded with jellyfish. That didn't deter them. They both swam with Jay coming in second place. Suni was eleven years old and Jay was fifteen.

✧

'At one time Suni went for a swim meet along with our friends, since we were camping. After the swim meet our friends brought Suni to the campground. We asked Suni: "How did you do at the swim meet?" She said 'Okay' and started playing with the other children. She must have been six or seven years old. We looked in her bag. There were five medals for the different events in which she came first. This is Suni's characteristic nature. She is always humble,' Bonnie says modestly.

✧

'Once we were on the beach at Cape Cod. Suni was six years old. She made a big sand castle. She asked us to come and have a look. We saw the well-done sand castle, but were very much surprised to see the word "Ram" written in Hindi on the castle. Although I told the children the stories of the *Ramayana* and the *Mahabharata,* they had never been exposed to Hindi writings. It maybe that she remembered the word "Ram" from the book. The incident still amazes me.

✧

'We remember once we went to New Hampshire to ski. My mother came with us. Suni and mom went cross-country skiing while the rest of us went downhill skiing. Mom fell down and broke her finger. Jay, Dina and Suni just couldn't do enough for her. She (mom) always loved being with us since it was always an adventure. A photographer came and took a picture of Grandma and Suni cross-country skiing for his newspaper.

✧

'The first time we got our camper we took a trip to Mt. Madanock in the western part of MA. We didn't arrive until nightfall so we had a hard time putting the camper together. Finally, we did it with the help of a guide who had a spotlight. The following day, we decided to climb up the mountain. Mom was a good sport and came along with us. Jay took the backpack and climbed ahead. We were all behind and kind of angry with him since he had all the food and water. We were all thirsty so we sat by a stream and drank some water. Every time we met someone coming down the mountain we asked how far it was to the top. Only five minutes they would say. On and on we went and finally mom was almost ready to give up. Suni and Dina helped her and encouraged her to continue and finally we reached the summit. There was Jay with all the food. He felt sorry for forging ahead,' Deepak recounts.

Needham High School

Growing up in Needham influenced Sunita tremendously. 'I think I am a smart aleck because I grew up close enough to Boston and most people from Massachusetts speak fast.

'I think growing up there, it just becomes commonplace that you feel like everybody around you is going to college: [so] I'm going to go to college. That is never a question in your mind because there are so many universities, hospitals around that just tap into your interest.'

Sunita passed out of Needham High School in 1983. She excelled in math and science though she admits that she was 'not absolutely number one, I was just okay'. That is an understatement as she always stood high in class rank in all the subjects. And she won hundreds of medals for swimming.

In high school, Sunita was always one of the best swimmers on the team so everyone looked to her to win the race. She also travelled to Italy, Canada and Mexico with the swim team and this was a real exciting experience for the high school kids.

She was invited to join a sorority in high school where their main function was volunteer service in the community. She taught swimming to physically challenged children at summer camp. Suni was a 'Brownie' and a Girl Scout and helped to raise money for charitable organisations by swim-a-thons, and walk-a-thons for her town.

Her favourite activities around this time were soccer, swimming, horseback riding, and playing the piano, as well as baking and cooking with her mother.

As her parents say, 'She had a wonderful childhood. Lots of hard work. Always busy. No time to get into trouble. Always learning new things and always a new adventure. I would say it was the best time of all our lives. She had a most friendly nature, she had many friends, she concentrated on her studies and always excelled. She was always ready to help others and enjoyed camping and exploring new places. She was highly admired by her school teachers and friends throughout her life in Needham.'

The town of Needham, where Suni grew up, has decided to dedicate a children's playground in Suni's honour with spaceships, and space paraphernalia and also the books that Suni read as a child, such as *The Little Engine That Could*; *Curious George and the Rocket Ship*, etc.

Man's best friends . . . and the Pandyas'

There were always pets around the house. Sunita was just five when she got her first dog, a collie named Lassie, for Christmas. One of her pups, a tri-colour, was promptly named Bonjo, after their mother Bonnie and grandmother, Josephine. When the kids went to college, Bonnie decided to gift them a lovely black Labrador retriever, Sassy. However, Sunita's own first Labrador was Sassy's pup, a chocolate coloured Labrador, Chirpy. Little Chirpy needed company, so in came Turbo, a black Lab-retriever, which Sunita got as a gift for her husband. Coal was an apt name for another black Labrador, which Sunita and her sister Dina got for their mother from a breeder in Cape Cod. On Christmas Day, 2005, Sunita and her mother gifted Dina with a yellow Lab-retriever, Elsie, got from the same Cape Cod breeder.

A cute six year-old Jack Russell terrier, fondly referred to as 'Sunita's mistake'—as it was the only small dog in the family and a non-collie or Labrador—is her favourite Gorby, whose picture Sunita took with her to the ISS.

17

Water

Jay Pandya, Sunita's brother, graduated from the United States Naval Academy (USNA) the very year she passed out of high school. She had done well in her studies and could have enrolled in prestigious Ivy League universities, but she chose to go to the academy.

As Bonnie remembers: 'We were all going to the USNA graduation, but Suni wanted to stay home to finish up some things. Later, we learned she wanted to have a high school graduation party for her friends. Her friends were all were very good kids and well behaved and responsible. They had a great time. She had everyone take off their shoes before they entered the house. No one complained about noise or anything. The following day she flew down to Maryland and we celebrated Jay's graduation. We think Suni would have loved to become a veterinarian, but at the Naval Academy other opportunities and career options presented themselves and she took advantage of them. We still think that someday she might work with animals because she has a special bond with them.'

USNA is an institution for the undergraduate education of officers of the United States Navy and Marine Corps and is in Annapolis, Maryland, near Washington D.C. It also proudly claims that it has 'produced more astronauts than any other institution in the nation'.

Sunita made an impact even before her classes officially started. During the summer, when she had enrolled as a first year student (plebe) at the academy, she was recognised as an outstanding athlete and was given a special highest endurance award. She got to wear a distinctive T-shirt, noting this accomplishment. At the academy she was an achiever, though never a topper.

As her parents recall: 'At the academy you usually study engineering. Few study pre-med, or naval architecture, but Suni wanted to become a naval architect. Due to her many extracurricular commitments including running cross-country and track and swimming competitively (where she was voted captain of the team in her senior year), she was unable to succeed in the major and became a general science major at the academy.

'She tried but failed at what she really wanted at the time. This is one of the things she tries to stress on young kids. If you fail, it is not so bad, just keep trying and eventually you will succeed, maybe not at what you set out to do but maybe something even better! She graduated as one of the fifty or so women in a class of one thousand. It was not easy even to attend the USNA as a woman in 1983, so we give her a lot of credit for that accomplishment.'

Climbing a Greased Monument

The Herndon Monument, located in the academy, was commissioned by the officers of the US Navy as a tribute to Commander William Lewis Herndon (1813-1857) after he lost his life in the Pacific Mail steamer *Central America* during a hurricane off the coast of North Carolina on 12 September 1857. As per the age-old rule of the sea, in which the captain cannot abandon his ship in danger, Herndon gave up his life to save his fellowmen. The monument was erected at its present location on 16 June 1860 and has never been moved since, even though the academy was completely reconstructed later.

Every year as part of the year-end festivities, it is covered with lard and the 'plebes' attempt to climb the monument, remove a 'dixie cup' (the cap that plebes traditionally wore) and put a hat on top. This marks the successful completion of their first year.

Sunita was the only woman in her class that the men allowed to climb up the greased monument to try to get the dixie cup. She made it halfway up before they pulled her back, but it was all done in a spirit of camaraderie.

Sunita's close friends at the academy included Michael J. Williams (now her husband), Heidi Moser, Debbie Klatt, Vicky Webster and Ron Harris. 'The three girls, Heidi, Debbie and Vicky, were Suni's roommates at the academy and bridesmaids at her wedding. They came to her surprise fortieth birthday party here on Cape Cod. They supported each other through thick and thin at the academy where they were some of the very few women who attended the school.'

Ron Harris is a world-class runner who is now Director of Athletics at the academy. He organised a number of people from Maryland to run the Boston Marathon along with Suni and her sister Dina. He had his students make up a plaque for Suni, supporting her as 'Suni's Earth Support Team'.

Meeting Michael, Marrying Michael

The United States Naval Academy shaped Sunita's life in many ways. She met Michael Williams, who was her classmate there. He became her best friend and is now 'her beloved husband of eighteen years'.

Sunita graduated from the academy with a B.S., Physical Science degree. She received her commission as an Ensign in the United States Navy from the United States Naval Academy in May 1987.

Sunita and Michael got married soon after. The nuptials took place at St. Joseph's Church, Woods Hole, Cape Cod, a church that dates back to, and has the distinction of, being the oldest Mary Garden or a garden dedicated to Mother Mary.

Deepak nostalgically recollects: 'I distinctly remember that fine sunny day of their wedding. All the flowers bloomed with jubilant flavour, colour and fragrance and all the birds sang ever so more clearly their sweet songs with joy. Many friends and relatives from many parts of the US, Europe, Australia and India were present to celebrate this auspicious day. The heavens were delighted on that occasion to see their precious child who would reach their shore in the near future.'

Professionally, Sunita got a six-month temporary assignment at the Naval Coastal System Command, where she received her designation as a Basic Diving Officer and then reported to Naval Aviation Training Command to train as a pilot.

'I think she fell into flying. You can either go surface line, navy air, marines or submarine after graduation from the US Naval Academy. Then there are a few special options like a navy diver. She wanted to go to be a navy diver but there was only one billet for that position and of course the people at the top of their class got to pick what they wanted to do first. Since she didn't get navy diver she chose navy air. As she had to wait for the slot to open in

Pensacola, FL, she stayed at the USNA until the slot opened, doing some office work. In the meantime, the dive community invited her to come down and work with them while she waited to go the Pensacola for the air training,' says her father.

Most pilots, naturally, desire to fly fighter jets, but that was not to be for her. 'At that time, women weren't flying combat airplanes, so there were only a couple of billets for women. I didn't get my first choice—I got my second choice, which was helicopters,' says Sunita.

'I bring up all these little failures because it's one of those things that I tell kids that maybe you want something, but you get something else, but if you make the best of it, things sorta work out.'

Naval Aviator

Sunita was designated a Naval Aviator in July 1989. As her father proudly says: 'She went to Panama City, FL and did so well they offered her a slot as a navy diver. She then decided to go to navy air so now she has two designations, Navy Diver and Navy Aviator. As an aside, the training she did as a navy diver helped her succeed in the astronaut core at NASA for a couple of reasons. First, as a diver you learn to become very comfortable moving around underwater (practising your buoyancy) with just an oxygen tank to sustain you and second, as part of a navy diver's job, you learn to work underwater, fixing things, soldering, tightening bolts, etc. This experience is very similar to what the astronauts do to practise for weightlessness and tasks on their spacewalks.'

Sunita then reported to Helicopter Combat Support Squadron 3 for the initial H46, Seaknight training. Upon completion of this training, she was assigned to Helicopter Combat Support Squadron 8 in Norfolk, Virginia, and made overseas deployments to the Mediterranean, Red Sea and the Persian Gulf in support of Desert Shield and Operation Provide Comfort.

In September 1992, she was the officer-in-charge of an H46 detachment sent to Miami, Florida, for Hurricane Andrew Relief Operations, on board the USS *Sylvania*.

Sunita was selected for United States Naval Test Pilot School and began the course in January 1993. After graduation in December 1993, she was assigned to the Rotary Wing Aircraft Test Directorate as an H46 Project Officer, and V-22 Chase Pilot in the T-2.

Flying a helicopter during one of her field trips, Sunita went down to Johnson Space Centre. She and a couple of other helicopter pilots sat in the back while all the jet pilots in her Test Pilot School class were sitting in the front, listening to veteran astronaut, John Young, talk about the space shuttle and about flying to the moon. When Young mentioned he learned to fly a copter in order to land the Lunar Lander, it caught her attention.

Something clicked in her head and she realised that there *was* use for helicopter pilots in a journey to the moon. The thought evolved: 'The only one who's telling me I'm not going to be an astronaut is me.'

While there, she was also assigned as the squadron Safety Officer and flew test flights in the SH-60B/F, UH-1, AH-1W, SH-2, VH-3, H-46, CH-53 and the H-57. In December 1995, she went back to the Naval Test Pilot School as an instructor in the Rotary Wing department and the school's Safety Officer. There she flew the UH-60, OH-6 and the OH-58. From there she was assigned to the USS *Saipan* (LHA-2), Norfolk, Virginia, as the Aircraft Handler and the Assistant Air Boss.

Selected for the Astronaut Programme

However, the space bug had bitten Sunita. She researched on what was required, got her master's degree and applied. 'And, lo and behold, the second application, I got an interview. So, I think I'm very, very lucky,' she says.

Sunita was deployed on board the USS *Saipan* when she was selected for the astronaut programme in 1998. She has logged over 2,300 flight hours in more than thirty different aircraft.

'So, in this way, her career led her into flying and then out to the fleet after she got her wings and then on to Test Pilot School in Pax River, VA and then to NASA and the astronaut core. I think if she ever retires from NASA or the military, she just might go back to school and become a vet, or a teacher, and have a farm. She is also thinking of continuing with the space programme and of taking part in a mission to the moon, if the opportunity were to come up,' says Deepak.

Air

The visit to NASA had been the immediate provocation but the yearning to go higher and further, into space, goes back to her childhood. When Sunita was around five years old, she saw Neil Armstrong walk on the moon and thought: 'Wow! That's cool.' She would watch TV shows about space travel with fascination.

'President Kennedy had a great push for space travel. We watched this on TV and the first time man was on the moon and all the interesting things that were happening at that time—she was very in tune to all that. It is probably something that she had in the back of her mind,' says Bonnie.

There are hundreds of thousands of pilots and scientists out there in the wide world, but there are only about a hundred astronauts. Sunita wanted to try to become an astronaut. Says she: 'In my mind, I used to think everybody wants to be an astronaut. I've sort of found out now that maybe that's not so true.

'I never really thought that it would happen in my life. It seemed too far out there, something that I could never achieve.'

The Door to her Dream

Sunita began her training with NASA in the year 1998 and the very same year she was selected to work on the space station project.

To better acquaint herself with the Russian side of the mission, she spent considerable time in Moscow, at the Russian Space Agency, working with the crew of the first expedition to the ISS.

The work was tough and taxing. Physical tasks and endurance were coupled with an in-depth study of technical and engineering details. The initial training commenced with orientation briefings and tours, followed by scientific and technical briefings. Then came intensive instruction in Shuttle International Space Station Systems, physiological training and ground school. Sunita spent much of the time for preparation for her space odyssey learning about their side of the mission, their spacecraft, apart from imbibing the all-important knowledge of their land and their language, their customs and their culture.

Unknown and Unfathomable

Space, as we all know, is a huge void, so what can you really train for? Earthbound missions can more easily anticipate situations: they are based on the physical environment, the surroundings, and ground realities. But space? How does one really prepare for the great unknown? Simulation, after all, is partly based on experience and some amount of anticipation, but can it ever be like a training programme on earth?

Yet, the experience of previous crews, technology to foresee and anticipate situations, and finally, the immense power of the human mind to peer into the future, all go into the making of the highly intensive training schedule that Sunita Williams went through. T-38 flight training, water and wilderness survival techniques were all part of the exhaustive process.

Hi-tech Automation

According to her, Friday would be the day for receiving weekly training schedules. These included basic systems of the two sides of the ISS. Orientation of the space station, where she would be required to spend so much time, was a crucial aspect, with emphasis on heating systems, energy control and regulation, power and motion control. Also, we must remember that the ISS comprised two essentially different parts—the Russian side and the American side—and she was required to be thoroughly familiar with both.

Robotics forms a very important aspect of space travel and stay, since movement is restricted and human interaction or involvement is impossible in such a complicated and sophisticated array of instrumentation. Sunita had to undergo special and intensive training in the Robotics Branch of the ISS in what is technically termed 'Special Purpose Dexterous Manipulation'.

Just as we train and study everyday in our own specialities and vocations, with a set curriculum, so it is with space training. Simulated situations of everyday life aboard the space station are created and the experiences recorded, recreated and practised to perfection. The way we learn to deal with life's problems, emergencies and malfunctions, so it is aboard the ISS as the training enables and empowers the astronaut to deal with, and control, such occurrences. In our educative career we learn to construct, repair and add, and similarly did Sunita learn, since the space station is a progressive, on-going project.

The World is but an Oyster

During her rigorous preparations, Sunita had to undergo several assembly tasks and flying trainer jets was just one of them. Apart from everyday life being duplicated, there were the emergencies to be accounted for and these were time and again simulated to let her get the 'feel' of handling difficult situations with controlled calm. The course of her preparation led her to interact with experts from different parts of the world—as widely spread as Russia, Canada, Brazil and even Japan. This breaking down of barriers has become such an integral part of life today, even for us on earth.

Water Baby

Walking in space has long been considered akin to walking in water. This, Sunita had to do, time and again, not in comfortable swimwear, but in a bulky spacesuit. She was always a keen swimmer and had ambitions of a sports career, but would she have ever guessed that her liking for water would result in her stay underwater for nine days?

Sunita performed this feat in the Aquarius, National Oceanic and Atmospheric Administration's undersea laboratory for the NASA's Extreme Environments Mission Operations (NEEMO) as a new member of NEEMO '02. The unusual environment of the Aquarius makes it an ideal training facility for future spaceflight.

Sunita Williams, in her preparation for a space sojourn of just over six months, spent an agonising, rigorous and disciplined training for a period of eight years.

Space

After the space shuttle was launched with the crew of STS-116 on 9 December 2006, Sunita arrived at the ISS on 11 December 2006.

She woke up on her first morning to the strains of the famous Beatles song '*Here comes the sun*'. Time passed, but certainly not slowly for Sunita, on the space station. She could take three holidays a week, but these were generally rotated to suit the multi-ethnic crew. Nor was life without its moments of fun. Her experiments in space started with testing her culinary prowess at making sushi, but in the weightlessness, the wasabi (paste) got splattered everywhere and she had quite a time cleaning up. Now since the training manuals don't mention anything about how to clean up flying wasabi, obviously her lack of experience showed. The spicy greenish condiment was squirted out of a tube while Sunita was trying to use it with bag-packaged salmon.

Each of the three space station crew members is given a certain number of bonus packs of their favourite foods to help endure their months in space. Since everything is weightless, spilled food is no ordinary clean-up challenge. 'We finally got the wasabi smell out after it was flying around everywhere,' Sunita was to tell her mother later. 'We cleaned it up off the walls a little bit.' Unfortunately for her, the wasabi tube was banished to a cargo vehicle where it stayed packed away. A wistful Sunita said later, 'I don't think we're going to use it anymore. It's too dangerous.'

International Space Station

The ISS is located in an orbit round the earth at an approximate altitude of 360 kilometres and it travels at an average speed of 27,744 kilometres per hour, completing 15.7 orbits around the earth each day. From the date of its launch, on 20 November 1998, till the time Sunita Williams went aboard it, the ISS has completed over 46,000 orbits round the earth.

It is a joint project undertaken primarily by five space agencies: National Aeronautics and Space Agency, Russian Federal Space Agency, Japan Aerospace Exploration Agency, Canadian Space Agency, and the European Space

Agency. The Brazilian Space Agency and the Italian Space Agency work on separate contracts with NASA, with the latter operating outside the framework of the ESA. The legalities for the International Space Station were decided through an international treaty signed on 28 January 1998, by fifteen governments including the US, Canada, Japan, and the Russian Federation and eleven member states of the ESA.

Building the ISS requires more than forty 'assembly' flights. Besides these and the 'utilisation' flights, around thirty Progress spacecraft flights are supposed to be supplying the logistics until 2010. Experimental equipment, fuel and consumables are being, and will be, delivered by all the vehicles travelling to the space station: the Shuttle, the Russian Progress, the European ATV (Automated Transfer Vehicle), and the Japanese HTV (H-II Transfer Vehicle). When the assembly is complete, the space station will approximately have a pressurised volume of 1,000 cubic metres, a mass of 400,000 kilograms, 100 kilowatts of power output, a 108.4 metres long truss, 74 metres long modules, and 6 crew members.

For the first time, an international space station will derive its electrical power from the sun, whose light is converted into electricity through the use of solar arrays, attached to its permanent truss structure. The ISS Environmental Control and Life Support System provides or controls elements such as atmospheric pressure, oxygen levels, water, and fire extinguishing, among other things. The atmosphere in the space station is given the highest priority by the support system, but the system also collects processes and stores water and waste used and produced by the crew. The use of activated charcoal filters is the primary method for removing byproducts of human metabolism from the air.

Other Team Members

Besides Sunita, the other members of the space mission were Mission Commander Mark Polansky, Pilot William Oefelein, Mission Specialist Nicholas Patrick, Lead Spacewalker Bob Curbeam and the representative of the European Space Agency, Christer Fuglesang.

From the start, Sunita was aware of the mixed ethnicity of the team and of her Indianness. This might have prompted her to quip: 'I am half-Indian and I have got, I am sure, a group of Indian people who are looking forward to seeing this second person of Indian origin flying up in space. So it's nice to know that everybody brings along with them a group of people from all over the world who get interested in space.'

For spiritual company, she carried with her to the ISS, a copy of the *Bhagvad Gita*, a small statue of Lord Ganesha and a letter written in Hindi by her father. 'My dad and I would always be there sitting together and he would bring his *Gita* and read it to me. As a child it did not confuse me. It gave me a greater understanding that religion is sort of all the same thing...'

Goan Kitchen, Punjabi Gourmet Delights

There is an interesting anecdote from a Goan restaurant owner in Cape Canaveral opposite the United Space Alliance: 'The crew of the next space shuttle mission, at the request of Sunita Williams, decided to have their lunch before lift off at *Taste of Goa* on 7 December 2006. Sunita requested him to make some boneless *tandoori* (roasted) chicken so that she could have it in space, along with the chapattis and *samosas* and stash of *imli* (tamarind) chutney and hot sauce that she planned to take...'

The Indianness got to the rest of the crew in space too when, during one of the regular get-togethers for dinner in the Russian segment service module, out came *saag paneer* and *chhole*, which were much appreciated by the rest of the crew, with a promise of *samosas* to follow soon. 'Maybe a little too hot for some, without rice, *roti* or *raita*,' Sunita said during a chat at an official US State Department website about her experiences in orbit. 'Hopefully I'll be getting some *samosas* before too long.' Sunita has several Indian dishes in her bonus container, including Punjabi *kadhi* with *pakora*—vegetable fritters topped with yoghurt and curry—and *mutter paneer*. The dishes are packaged to have a long shelf life in space.

'Psychologically, it's very important,' space station dietician Paula Hall said of the gourmet extras. 'It's really important to have variety, to have surprises. It's important to have food that makes you happy, that makes you smile.' The crew must certainly have had reasons to smile after tasting Indian *tandoori* delicacies.

Spacewalk Record

Exercise was a very important activity on the ISS and a daily regimen was essential to maintain bone and muscle in micro-gravity. Part of the routine was a mini-triathlon comprising twenty-five minutes of biking, twenty minutes (2.7 kilometres) of running and several laps of floating, very much akin to swimming, inside the craft. This was combined with lifting weights, and even grasping objects with the feet, to keep the muscles toned and healthy.

Walking, however, was not restricted to the inside of the space station for Sunita and the crew. On 16 December 2006 she, along with Bob Curbeam, moved outside the confines of the ISS. A tedious 7 hours and 31 minutes later, they had completed the rewiring of the International Space Station. Again, on 31st January and 4th & 9th February, Sunita completed three spacewalks with Michael Lopez-Alegria, with the third lasting 6 hours 40 minutes.

Sunita Williams, by then, had registered a total of 29 hours and 17 minutes in spacewalks, surpassing the record held by Kathryn C. Thornton for the maximum spacewalk time by a woman astronaut.

Wearing a Navy T-shirt bearing race number 14,000 and strapped down to the treadmill by a painful harness, she completed the gruelling race in 4 hours 24 minutes. In the process, she actually travelled 121,600 kilometres, or almost thrice round the world. While she watched the event on earth through a laptop, in an act of kinship, her sister Dina completed the marathon on ground, along with fellow NASA astronaut Karen Nyberg.

Her spacewalk was a truly unique experience. Said an astonished Sunita: 'I was amazed that you can look all around 360 degrees and see everything, and to really see the whole horizon, the curvature of the earth and all the stars as well, was just spectacular, and while we were out there we had the opportunity to see the Aurora, the Northern Lights, and that was just a little bit creepy because it was this green shadow thing coming over the earth. It was pretty spectacular, and I think the others were also pretty amazed at that type of view.' Floating around in space and looking outside, according to her, refreshed her geography lessons. Nor did she forget history in the making, in the country of her origin for on Thursday, 11 January 2007 she sent a message of congratulations to the Indian space scientists on the successful launch of the PSLV.

No Barriers of Space and Time

Ham radio operators were permitted to speak to the astronauts and she spent time talking to people living as far apart as New York, Australia and California. Just imagine this: He is over three kilometres under water; she is 345 kilometres up in the atmosphere. They both work in small, confined spaces, looking out onto vast, unpopulated expanses. He is out of the reach of sunlight, buried under a blanket of perpetual darkness; she watches sunrise fifteen times a day…if she has enough time to look for it!

Both are explorers of the last frontiers. Tim Shanks, underwater explorer and Sunita Williams, space traveller, shared their individual experiences on 27 January 2007, through radio. During their fifteen-minute conversation, the pair answered questions from students, educators and the public. 'Greetings Alvin, this is the International Space Station Alpha, flying about 250 miles above the earth's surface,' Williams began.

One question was about what alien life forms each had seen so far in their separate environments. 'We haven't seen anything up here, but I'm sure you've seen stuff that looks pretty weird down there,' said Sunita. 'Yes, absolutely Suni,' said Shanks, 'some of the life forms down here…I think of as being aliens. We're both living life in the extremes.' At times, the two showed signs of 'status' envy.

'Hey, what do you think about switching jobs?' Sunita asked. 'I'd love to do your job and see what's living on the ocean floor. How about coming up here sometime?' 'I would love to do that,' Shanks said.

Answering Questions

Twenty-four Grade IV & V students from the 'Gifted and Talented' education programme at Dilworth Elementary School sat jittering with nerves and excitement, via amateur radio, to ask Sunita Williams, one question each. Some of the questions and their answers were most interesting.

Q: What is the most impressive scene in outer space?

A: I think the most impressive scene up here is actually seeing the whole planet; it's pretty impressive. We live in a beautiful place.

Q: What advice would you give to kids following in your footsteps?

A: I think if anybody wants to be an astronaut, they can be. A couple things to keep in mind: pick a job that you like or an occupation that you like, and do it well. We are looking for all types of occupations to be astronauts. Secondly, keep yourself in good health.

Q: How long does it take to get to the International Space Station?

A: It took about eight and a half minutes to get to space but about two days to get to the space station because we had to line up for our rendezvous between the two spacecrafts and that takes a little bit of time.

Q: If you can, give us a bit of advice for future astronauts.

A: One bit of advice is, be adventurous, but again stay healthy and remember not to take your health for granted. Always try to learn new things and you will go very far.

Happy New Year

New Year Eve is always a special occasion, wherever you are on earth, and it was no different for the ISS crew in outer space. 'We saw the moon—almost full, behind us on New Year Eve,' said an excited Sunita. The event prompted her to make a poetic entry in the space station's logbook:

It's January 1, 2007
We look out the window and realise we are the closest humans to heaven

We look at the earth and it's not hard to believe
What those billions of folks down there can achieve

Our thoughts wander to the explorers of the past
So many hardships and sacrifices to make the moulds they cast

The fruit of their labour is that we sail a ship of golden solar arrays
Along a path that is constant and stays

Today's achievement is a result of cooperation and friendship around the world
The faces, the language, the flags—all swirled

Like so many others before us, we dedicate our lives
In hopes that the future of humanity thrives

Here's to the future generation of explorers, you are our motivation
To continue to explore as one combined nation

April Fool

Sunita Williams also tested a miniature biological laboratory for the first time onboard the International Space Station. The mini-lab is called LOCAD-PTS (Lab-On-a-Chip Application Development-Portable Test System) and detects the presence of bacteria or fungi on the surfaces of a spacecraft far more rapidly than standard methods of culturing. The LOCAD-PTS is designed so that astronauts can do the analysis onboard with no need to return samples to laboratories on earth.

On 31 March 2007, Sunita assembled the LOCAD-PTS components and took several readings. The first two were to verify that the instrument was working properly. Then,

Some of the 1998 astronaut candidate class that included Sunita Williams lined up for a photo while standing under the engines of the Saturn V rocket on display.

Astronaut Sunita Williams.
A NASA portrait in EMU suit used for spacewalk
or EVA (Extra-Vehicular Activity).

The STS-116 crew portrait. Front row (from left), astronauts William A. Oefelein, Pilot; Joan E. Higginbotham, Mission Specialist; and Mark L. Polansky, Commander. On the back row (from left) are astronauts Robert L. Curbeam, Nicholas J.M. Patrick, Sunita Williams and European Space Agency's Christer Fuglesang, all Mission Specialists.

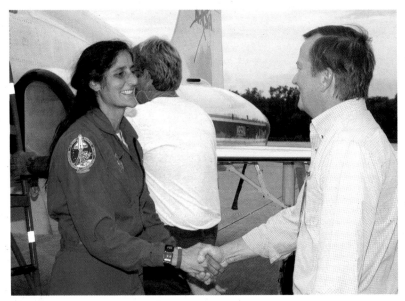

At the Shuttle Landing Facility, Launch Director Mike Leinbach (right) welcomes
STS-116 Mission Specialist Sunita Williams upon her arrival at KSC aboard a
T-38 jet aircraft for the launch of Space Shuttle Discovery on 7 December 2006.

Crew members of mission STS-116 gather around the table for breakfast before
suiting up for launch aboard Space Shuttle Discovery. From left are Mission
Specialist Nicholas Patrick, Pilot William Oefelein, Mission Specialist Joan
Higginbotham, Commander Mark Polansky, and Mission Specialists
Sunita Williams, Robert Curbeam and Christer Fuglesang.

STS-116 Mission Specialists Sunita Williams (left) and Joan Higginbotham listen to instructions on use of the M-113 armoured personnel carrier that could be used to move them quickly away from the launch pad in the event of an emergency.

Mission Specialist Sunita Williams helmeted and ready to practise driving the M-113 armoured personnel carrier.

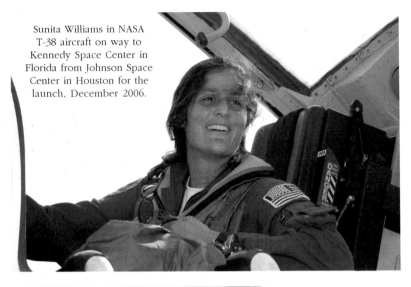

Sunita Williams in NASA T-38 aircraft on way to Kennedy Space Center in Florida from Johnson Space Center in Houston for the launch, December 2006.

Mission Specialists Christer Fuglesang, and Sunita Williams check out the port integrated truss structure, P5, which is the primary payload on their mission.

The STS-116 crew pause in their pre-launch activities to talk to the media at Launch Pad 39B.

Crew members gather for a photo in front of the white solid rocket boosters and external tank of Space Shuttle Discovery. From left are Commander Mark Polansky, Pilot William Oefelein and Mission Specialists Nicholas Patrick, Robert Curbeam, Christer Fuglesang, Joan Higginbotham and Sunita Williams.

Sunita is helped by the closeout crew in the White Room to secure her launch suit before climbing into Discovery.

In the white room on Launch Pad 39B, Sunita Williams is helped with her gear before entering Space Shuttle Discovery.

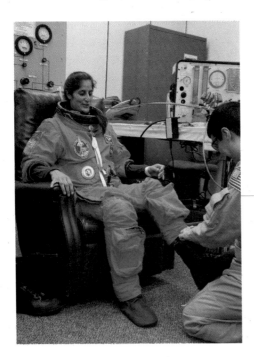

Mission Specialist Sunita Williams is helped with her boot before heading to Launch Pad 39B.

Sunita Williams suiting up for a second launch attempt aboard Space Shuttle Discovery. The first launch attempt of STS-116 on 7 December 2006 was postponed due a low cloud ceiling over Kennedy Space Center.

This fish-eye view shows the water flooding the mobile launcher platform as Space Shuttle Discovery lifts off Launch Pad 39B on mission STS-116.

Viewed through the leaves of a tree in the foreground, the fiery liftoff of
Discovery on mission STS-116 lights up the nearby water.
This was Discovery's 33rd mission and the first night launch since 2002.

Astronaut Sunita Williams, participating in the mission's third planned session of extravehicular activity (EVA) as construction resumed on the International Space Station on 16 December 2006. The spacewalk lasted 7 hours, 31 minutes.

Wg. Cdr. Rakesh Sharma, the first Indian to go into space, at the American Centre, New Delhi where Sunita Williams interacted with school students and journalists.

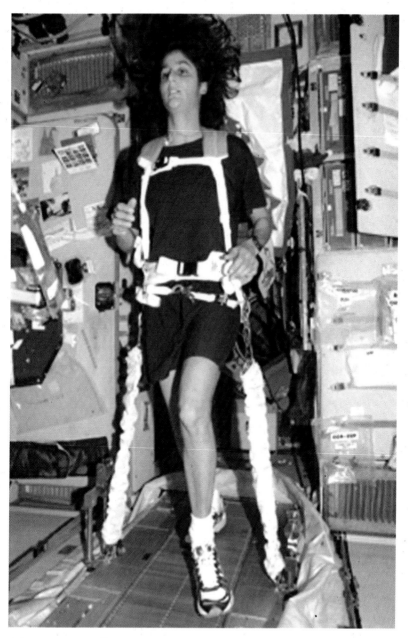

Astronaut Sunita Williams, Expedition 14 Flight Engineer, equipped with a bungee harness, exercises on the Treadmill Vibration Isolation System (TVIS) in the Zvezda Service Module of the International Space Station on 28 December 2006.

Flashing a thumbs up sign here, astronaut Sunita Williams circled the Earth almost three times as she participated in the Boston Marathon on 16 April 2007. She ran at about six miles per hour while flying more than five miles each second, as she completed the marathon on a station treadmill. Sunita's official completion time was 4 hours, 23 minutes and 10 seconds.

A group portrait of STS-117 and Expedition 15 crew members.
From the left (front row) are astronauts Clayton Anderson, Expedition 15 Flight
Engineer; Sunita Williams, STS-117 Mission Specialist; Cosmonauts Fyodor N.
Yurchikhin and Oleg V. Kotov, Expedition 15 Commander and Flight Engineer,
respectively, representing Russia's Federal Space Agency.
From the left (middle row) are astronauts Lee Archambault and Rick Sturckow,
STS-117 Pilot and Commander, respectively.
From the left (back row) are astronauts Patrick Forrester, Jim Reilly,
Steven Swanson and John "Danny" Olivas, all STS-117 Mission Specialists.

Space Shuttle Atlantis is backdropped by a blue and white Earth as it approaches
the International Space Station during STS-117 rendezvous and docking operations
on 10 June 2007. A pair of solar arrays and starboard truss segments can be seen in
Atlantis' cargo bay. A docked Soyuz spacecraft is visible at top centre.

Returning from mission STS-117, Space Shuttle Atlantis approaches touchdown on the runway at NASA's Dryden Flight Research Center at Edwards Air Force Base in California. Atlantis landed on orbit 219 after 13 days, 20 hours and 12 minutes in space. The landing was diverted to California due to marginal weather at the Kennedy Space Center. Main gear touchdown was at 3:49:38 p.m. EDT on runway 22. Nose gear touchdown was at 3:49:49

Media and staff in the NASA News Center at Kennedy Space Center applaud the successful landing of Atlantis, visible on the television screens, at NASA's Dryden Flight Research Center at Edwards Air Force Base in California.

she took readings of various objects around the cabin that could contain bacteria. The instrument showed a strong positive reading that, indeed, bacteria were being detected.

'The cleaner the sample, the longer the analysis takes,' confirmed the experiment's principal investigator, Mr Wainwright. 'Because this site was pretty clean, it took about twelve minutes, but dirty samples can take as little as a couple of minutes. The ability to monitor micro-organisms would be especially important on long space voyages, not only to check the health of astronauts but also to monitor electronics and structural materials, which can be corroded or otherwise damaged by certain fungi and bacteria,' he added.

However, it was actually past midnight on 1st April, Greenwich Mean Time, when Sunita said, 'Ah, this last set of readings for LOCAD-PTS looks a bit strange'. After a pause of about five seconds, she exclaimed, to the amusement of her team, 'Happy April Fools' Day! The numbers are just fine!'

With Mrs DiNapoli's class

She has kept in touch with students from Mrs Angela DiNapoli's class and here are some of the questions that she answered when she was quizzed from Babson College:

Q: What is your favourite food in space?

A: Peanut butter and marshmallow on a tortilla. It's my favourite on earth too!

Q: What do you miss the most?

A: My dog, Gorby, a Jack Russell terrier.

Q: What's one of the best things about being in space?

A: The fact that you never need to get a ladder to reach things; I can just sidle myself into the position I need, including 'standing' on my head if it helps.

Q: What have you learned while up there?

A: Earth is a large and beautiful body with no boundaries or dividing lines; it's hard to understand why anyone would argue about particular regions on this planet— let alone fight over them!

Proud Neighbours

Her neighbours are extremely proud of Sunita, say her parents. 'Many of them have attended the family conferences with Suni at our home. They are in awe of her being an astronaut and feel honoured to know an astronaut. They all say the same thing: "How down-to-earth she is! How easy it is to talk to her. How readily she shares her experiences with everyone. She has no airs about her."

'The people that know her say they are not surprised at her achievements. She was always shooting for the stars in everything she did. She is more remarkable because she is (seemingly) such an ordinary person who achieved such an extraordinary goal. In Boston and USA most of the people have been amazed at her accomplishment in the space station.'

Star

She is idolised by thousands of people all over the world; for her parents, she is a child they are proud of; her hometown Needham considers Sunita a distinguished citizen; many in India claim her as their own.

Who is Sunita Williams? Well, a regular person with extraordinary drive, discipline and determination.

Starting with the Regular

Bonnie, her mother tells us that bringing up Sunita was a pleasure because she was a very well behaved child. 'She never made a fuss about anything and always listened to my advice. We loved to go shopping together and at the end of the shopping trip I would go to our favourite candy store to buy her some candy. She was fun to be with and had a wonderful personality. We were always happy in each other's company.

'However, bringing up Sunita was also a pain because when she was a little baby, she could never sleep through the night. At the time, Dina was three years old and Jay was four years old. I would be exhausted taking care of the two older children and could hardly wait to go to sleep. As soon as I fed her and put her in her crib, I would go to sleep. No sooner would I fall asleep than Suni started crying. I would get up and walk with her and after she fell asleep I would put her back in her crib. Again, she would start crying. One day, after a particularly bad waking-sleeping night, I finally took her into my bed. She then fell soundly asleep. The next day we found out that the poor little thing had an ear infection.

'Suni had real long hair. She swam everyday twice a day, so her hair was always wet. Suni brushed the top and sides of her hair and the back was always in tangles. I tried to gently comb it out but she didn't like it and wanted to do it herself. I think she had tangled hair for quite some time. This was the only troublesome thing about Suni. Otherwise, she was a real pleasure.'

Does not like Scary Movies

Deepak, her father, tells us that her favourite food is spaghetti and meat balls, peanut butter and fluff, pizza, ice cream, macaroni and cheese, tomato soup, bagels, cream cheese and salmon, *samosas, gulab jambun*, jams and pickles, *kadhi pakoras, pani puri, dal-dhokree, sevaiya, ras malai,* and all kinds of *sabzi*, Indian breads like *roti, naan, paratha* and most Indian sweets. Bonnie has learnt to prepare all types of sweets and Indian foods for her family.

'I know she does not like to watch scary movies. She liked comedies, and animal and children's movies. In particular, we think she likes the message the children's movies give to kids in a fun way. I think she tries to do this when she is talking to kids from space.

'Every holiday when she returned from school she would watch Christmas shows and comedies. I can't think of any fears she has other than scary things.'

The Pandya children had a normal relationship with each other, say their parents. 'There was some fighting between the two older children since they were only thirteen months apart. Suni was four years younger than Jay and three years younger than Dina. Suni got along well with both Jay and Dina, who were good role models for her. They all studied hard, did well in school and spent much of their free time at swimming practice and at swim meets, which made all of them extremely well organised and efficient at managing their time.

Followed her Brother to the Naval Academy

Jay chose to go to the Naval Academy first and then Suni decided to follow in his footsteps. The first class to have women graduates was the Class of 1979 and these women were seniors when Jay was a plebe or freshman. He wasn't very happy to have women at a military academy but he told Suni that if there were going to be women there, she might as well be one of them because he was sure she would do well. Being four years apart, Jay graduated in 1983 while Suni entered the academy the same year and graduated in 1987.

'After Jay got his driver's license he would drive Suni and Dina to swimming practice. I was working at the time so he would walk over to my work and take my car so they would all be able to go to practice.'

When Jay was stationed in San Diego as a Naval Officer, he invited Suni to come out and go skiing with him. They had a wonderful time together. When he was stationed in Hawaii he invited Dina to stay with him for a while and they also had a great time. Jay was always loving and wanted to share his life with his sisters.

Brotherly Love and Poison Ivy

Jay got a sports car when he graduated from the USNA. He was going to be in the Philippines for three years, so he decided to give it to Suni. She loved the car, but unfortunately, she got into an accident with it. In her junior year at the USNA, they had a ring dance where the students get their rings and dip it into the water from the seven seas.

It is a big event and the students usually invite a special person to go with them to the dance. Suni invited her father. He was all set to go when he got a call from her telling him she was not going to the ring dance.

Her parents found out later that she went over an embankment with the car and landed in a patch of poison ivy. She was unhurt but was full of poison ivy. Her face was so swollen that she could not even see. Her sponsor at the USNA called them to tell them what had happened to her. That was the end of her sports car. Fortunately, she came out of it just fine.

Discipline drove her on

Dina remembers this about her younger sister: 'I think the main influences on Sunita during her childhood and teens were the discipline from sports. She realised at an early age that she had to work hard to achieve. She always had to swim the long distance events like the 1650, 500, 400, Individual Medley, etc. Other swimmers won their events swimming a twenty-five or a fifty-yard free while Suni did the endurance events. She didn't always win but gained the respect from her peers. Our whole family was always busy.

Our neighbours used to say, "Don't you people ever stay home? We get tired just watching you come and go".'

Suni saw her brother and sister working hard and wanted to be like them. The children were all strong and healthy and combined with their willingness to work and their ability to achieve, they were all outstanding students and athletes.

A Challenge called Life

'Her greatest triumph was to complete the Boston Marathon when she was a junior in high school. It was a warm spring day and Suni and I were out working in the yard. It was the day of the Boston Marathon and we were listening to the news media on the radio. She asked me if I would take her to the start. I agreed, so we jumped in the car and I drove her to the start about twenty miles away. She did not train for the marathon, her only training was swimming and the running the coach had them do before practice. She had old boy high-top shoes on and I gave her ten cents to call me in case she got stuck somewhere.

'I was waiting at the halfway point in Wellesley, MA. After a couple hours she finally came by and took off her shoes saying her feet were killing her in the high-tops. She ran the rest of the way barefooted. About five hours it took her to complete the marathon; I was waiting for her at the finishing line. We took the train back to my car and I drove her home. It took her a couple days to recuperate from the event. I never thought she would do it but I sure did not want to discourage her. It just showed again how she could put her mind over matter to do something she was determined to do. I think that was her greatest triumph aside from becoming an astronaut and living in space for six months and doing four spacewalks.'

Sunita the Indian

Sunita's parents say that they made efforts to inculcate Indian values in her. Bonnie tells us: 'We often had Indian visitors come and stay with us from India. I always cooked Indian food for my husband since he is a vegetarian. We also had several swamis come and stay with us. We took the kids to India on a vacation when they were in high school and travelled all around. Sunita very much likes Indian food especially Indian snacks, *papad* and chutney.'

Sunita recollects: 'My mother would cook two different meals each day, one Indian and one meat and potatoes, so I got to eat a little bit of both and a good variety. I still like spicier food…'

The children liked listening to Indian music very much, recollects Bonnie: 'We went for Indian movies, musical performances and dance shows. We also made a point to take them to Indian spiritual meetings. Deepak also told them stories of Ram and Krishna during the long car rides at the time of trips. We went to India several times and travelled through many areas in Gujarat, especially Sabarmati Gandhi Ashram, Porbandar in Saurashtra, Rajasthan, Delhi, Agra, Ajanta, Ellora, Madras, Bangalore and Bombay. Thus, we visited Mahatma Gandhi's birthplace and the place where he departed from this world.

'During the visit to these two places, Deepak explained to the children what Gandhi meant to India and about his contribution to the world. Visiting these places we all had tears in our eyes. Sunita's visits to India has impressed in her Gandhi's message of truth, love and non-violence. Like Gandhi and Dad, she also leads a very simple life with a positive outlook. We also visited several of our relatives and we were overcome by their enormous affection and joy at seeing us in India.

'Sunita loved to sing Indian movie songs such as *Ichak Dana, Ichak Dana* . . . which she danced to when she was little girl. She also liked the song, *Kabhie, Kabhi.*'

Sunita has been to India thrice: once as a very small child, again in 1998 and for the third time after the Columbia crash. Back in her village in India, people were concerned. 'We are proud, but at the same time anxious for her safety. We are keeping our fingers crossed,' said Sunita's paternal uncle Denish Raval. A rally was organised at her ancestral village Julhason, Mehsana District. Said Raval, 'The entire village has been ceaselessly praying for her safety.' Nothing to wonder at, really.

He also relates an incident when she had visited Julhason as a small girl in the mid-1970s. 'After a camel ride, she insisted on taking the camel back home! The villagers talk of the incident even now!'

Kalpana Chawla: A Woman of the Universe

Sunita is the second woman astronaut of Indian origin after Kalpana Chawla, whose space odyssey came to a tragic end on 1 February 2003, when the space shuttle Columbia exploded over Texas during re-entry.

'Kalpana belonged to the universe,' was Sunita's deferential comment. Her visit to India after the death of Kalpana Chawla in the Columbia spacecraft tragedy was part of an effort by the Chawla family and others to keep alive the memory of the first Indian-American woman astronaut.

Sunita is quick to acknowledge that she learnt a lot from Kalpana: 'Just being with her was great fun.' 'Kalpana Chawla had a lot of different interests. One of her interests was in Indian music. And they both used to listen to Indian classical music together,' says Deepak.

'Suni developed a taste for Indian classical music from Kalpana, who gave tapes of the different ragas to her. She cherished listening to the music produced by various Indian musical instruments,' remembers Bonnie.

Sunita has this to say of Kalpana: 'She was a gracious and unassuming woman. We spent many leisure hours together, took innumerable bike rides, spent time looking at birds, or went on long hikes. And we often flew together in a small airplane.'

For Indians who continue to mourn the tragic death of Kalpana Chawla, Sunita Williams has become the living embodiment of her friend and colleague's dream. Her special message for the people of India is to dream like her for, 'if you believe in it, it will come true'!

Remarkable Parents

Deepak's résumé has a list of 121 publications, which he has either written or co-authored. He is still an active academician and a highly regarded neuroanatomist.

Bonnie's professional life took a backseat while she brought up the children and took care of the family. 'After the kids were old enough I started working and then went to get my degree in business administration. My final job was at Babson College where I was a programme coordinator for the entrepreneurship programme. I retired in 1995.'

The couple have lived on Cape Cod since that year and these days, Bonnie is writing a children's book titled *Gorbie and the Astronaut*, a story about Suni and her little Jack Russell terrier.

Even little dogs in that household have stories to tell!

Touchdown

Several things happened during the final days of Sunita Williams' stay aboard the International Space Station.

The launch of space shuttle Atlantis, that was to fetch her back to earth, was delayed due to technical snags. It finally docked with the ISS, but with a minute tear on its thermal shield, which although termed 'not dangerous', had to be repaired, especially in view of the tragic death of seven astronauts including Kalpana Chawla, when space shuttle Columbia broke up during re-entry in February 2003.

The Atlantis crew worked on the on-orbit construction of the station with the installation of the Starboard 3 & 4 truss segment, and conducted four spacewalks to activate the solar array. With this, twelve more construction missions would be needed to finish building the Space Station by the 2010 deadline.

Astronaut Danny Olivas, 'spacewalked' to stitch up the tear in the thermal blanket of Atlantis using surgical staples.

Computers on the Russian side of the ISS malfunctioned for an unprecedented forty-eight hours, seemingly due to the installation of solar arrays. Subsequently, the ISS crew used a jumper cable to bypass a faulty power switch to rectify the problem and let the computers run overnight.

With all this, the eleven-day mission of Atlantis was extended to thirteen days.

And Indian origin astronaut Sunita set yet another record, this time for the longest uninterrupted space flight by a woman, surpassing the 188-day-4-hour mark of her compatriot Shannon Lucid, set in 1996 on the Russian Space Station MIR. When asked what she was doing at the time, pat came her typically unassuming reply, "I had a couple of wrenches in my hand, or something."

After six years of people living in space on the ISS, three of them women, the 11-year record had been broken, that too on her maiden space flight. Shannon's reaction was extremely positive: "It was very exciting to watch her spacewalks and to watch her accumulate more spacewalk time than any other female in the Universe."

While on earth, her family, friends, colleagues and millions of unknown people awaited her arrival with bated breath and a prayer on their lips. In Ahmedabad, schoolchildren prayed for her safe return.

Nostalgia

She was looking forward to rain, a swim in the ocean, lake or a pool, even maybe just a shower or a bath. Contrary to normal expectation, life in space can make one feel quite dirty. In the weightlessness, sweat tends to cling to the skin, accumulates as globules that then get shaken off and float around till they bang into something.

At times, Sunita would be filled with an overwhelming urge to touch the earth. She would think of the early Apollo astronauts and how frustrated they might have felt at simply orbiting the moon and returning to earth without actually landing on the moon.

Eating food day after day out of a bag can be a terribly boring routine and the temptation to dig into a scoop of ice cream was great indeed. Her favourite delicacy being 340 km below, on land, she was keenly looking forward to pistachio ice cream with chocolate sauce.

As night drew near, the earth would begin to twinkle and areas that appeared barren by day would miraculously light up with tiny pinpricks. All this filled her with a longing to "feel and smell the spray of the sea on my face". She said: "I will be happy to come back to earth, our beautiful planet."

TOUCHDOWN

With all her experience and expertise, she still terms space flight dangerous. However, she hopes people would "follow in her footsteps". 'Float in her wake' would probably be more appropriate, since the lack of gravity in space allows one to work upright, upside down, sideways, any which way. In her own words, "Space is absolutely a 3-D world in comparison to our 2-D world on earth."

Agony, hope and ecstasy

The landing of the Atlantis was scheduled for 11.30 pm IST on Thursday, 21 June 2007 at the Kennedy Space Centre, Florida. The crew eagerly awaited the command from earth, to begin descent; that, however, was not to be. Weather was bad; there was a thick blanket of cloud at 8,000 feet and signs of an imminent storm. Re-entry was aborted. An agonising twenty-four hours later, the situation was the same.

Mankind prayed as one for the safe return of Sunita and the crew. Across India, there were images of candles and havens lit, and sounds of prayers and *bhajans*. The world breathed a collective sigh of relief when, finally, the space shuttle Atlantis, then cruising at an awesome speed of around 27,000 kmph, slowed down to a comparative crawl and entered the earth's atmosphere 40,000 feet above land, to touchdown safely at the Edwards Air Base, California, at 1.19 am IST.

Jubilation broke out in the streets of India, especially in Ahmedabad, the city of the Pandyas' origin and Karnal, the birthplace of Kalpana Chawla. With her return, Sunita had completed an incredible 194 days, 18 hours and 15 minutes in space.

The relief of the family was palpable, with Dr. Deepak Pandya going on air to specially thank the people of India who had diligently followed her space odyssey and who had prayed for her safe return.

Sunita Williams is truly a marathoner—the only space marathoner in the world. She is an achiever extraordinaire. What, then, would be the next frontier to cross? A 522-day trip to Mars? With Sunita Williams, there are no final frontiers, just new targets.

Bibliography

Initial information was drawn from the following websites:

1. Wikipedia.com
2. Nirali Magazine's interview with Sunita Williams as posted on wikipedia
3. rediff.com
4. NASA website
5. sify.com
6. Personal information and photographs are completely courtesy her family, compiled and sent by her sister Dina

Index